POCKE

Keswick and the Central Lakes

John Marsh

NONSUCH

This book is dedicated to the 'Poets, Artists, Bishops and Sentimentalists' of the

Thirlmere Defence Association, whose cause drowned one hundred years ago.

First published 1993
This new pocket edition 2007
Images unchanged from first edition

Nonsuch Publishing Limited
Cirencester Road, Chalford
Stroud, Gloucestershire, GL6 8PE
www.nonsuch-publishing.com

Nonsuch Publishing is an imprint of NPI Media Group

© John Marsh, 1993

The right of John Marsh to be identified as the Author
of this work has been asserted in accordance with the
Copyrights, Designs and Patents Act 1988.

British Library Cataloguing in Publication Data.
A catalogue record for this book is available from the British Library.

ISBN 978-1-84588-421-5

Typesetting and origination by NPI Media Group
Printed in Great Britain

Contents

A Rigg's of Windermere coach climbs out of Keswick towards Windermere, c. 1910.

Introduction

Guide books to the Keswick area in the late nineteenth and early twentieth centuries gave their readers details of the town and the surrounding countryside and this book generally follows their coverage. This was the area of the horse carriage drives from the popular tourist resort, with the odd foot, or horseback, excursion into the fells. By restricting the coverage to the guide books' boundaries it has been possible to present an illustrated guide to a very special area that has changed much in the decades since the photographs were taken.

The ancient importance of the valley of the Rivers Derwent and Greta is attested in the magnificent stone circle on the moorland between Briery and Castlerigg. The Romans undoubtedly came this way, as their forts and roads are all around, but scholars seek an actual site of Roman date in the Keswick valley.

In the early Christian period St Kentigern (or Mungo) and St Herbert knew the area well. There are a number of early Christian sites to be found. The pre-Norman church at Crosthwaite became part of a Manor held by the Ratcliffes, although rights to the church itself were given to Fountains Abbey by the Crown. The exploitation of the minerals of Borrowdale and the adjoining valleys dates back certainly to the Middle Ages and possibly to Roman times.

The family of the Earls of Derwentwater, as the Ratcliffes had become, married royalty when Edward Ratcliffe married Mary, illegitimate daughter of Charles II, but their son, the third Earl of Derwentwater, as was the way with many, lost his head for participating in the Jacobite attempt to gain the throne in 1715. His brother, who had escaped to France, shared the same fate in 1746 after supporting Bonny Prince Charlie.

In 1545 the historian Leland called Keswick 'a poor little market town', and so it remained until, with the advent of the 'Romantic' conception of the English Lake District, the town became known as 'the capital of the Lakes'. This transformation from poor backwater to fame in the tourists' itinerary was without doubt due to the improvement of access to the place. Poor tracks became roads suitable for horse transport, and the railway age added its own contribution in the form of the Cockermouth, Keswick and Penrith Railway which was opened in 1864/5. Crowds then flocked to the town, in spite of the records of annual rainfall, to make Keswick and the surrounding district, in the late Victorian and Edwardian periods, a prosperous resort. Some of this prosperity was shared by both local and national photographers and part of their work in the area during those 'boom' years can be glimpsed in the pages of this book. Even the cows and sheep, in a district famous for its poor farming conditions, were given a romantic tinge and featured in the photographic publicity aimed at the tourists.

At the centre of this photographic publicity for many years were the Abraham family. George Perry Ashley Abraham had come to Keswick in 1862 as an apprentice to Alfred Pettitt, Artist and Photographer. In 1866 young Abraham set up his own business and this was enlarged greatly when his two sons, George and Ashley, extended their father's rock scrambling into serious rock climbing and started to write books illustrated by themselves. Ashley became the first President of the Fell and Rock Climbing Club and Chairman of Keswick Council. The family gained an international reputation as climbing and mountain photographers. At the local level, however, Victorian and Edwardian Keswick and its tourism was the Abrahams' main commercial interest.

The Abrahams were not the only photographers in Keswick and it could be fairly argued that they were not the best. That they were the most prolific in the local tourist postcard business is without doubt. Over many decades they had printed, in various European printing works, multi-thousands of very poor reproductions of quite ordinary photographs for outletting through the many tourist interests with which they had an influence. They took the 'artistic' faking of photographs used by Pettitt into a completely new dimension, cutting and shaping their images to suit the requirements of the time. Not only did the same swans appear on many a lake but vehicles and people appeared against added backgrounds and the steepness of roads and fells were enhanced for effect. The 'fakery' of turn of the century photographers is a study in itself, and the Abrahams were masters of the craft. The other Keswick photographers also carried out fakery of their images but not to the extent that can be seen in a collection of Abraham photographs.

In this book readers will find the work of Alfred Pettitt, who had his famous studio and galleries in St John Street and was said to be the father of Lake District photography, and Henry Mayson, whose studio, originally centred on his relief model of the Lakes, was in Lake Road, as well as pictures by the Abrahams, also of Lake Road. Pettitt was undoubtedly the first of the trio to set up in business, to be followed by his pupil Abraham. Mayson, who did not open a studio until the 1880s, struggled to compete, in spite of his being a brilliant photographer, and so used his relief map, copied by the Abrahams, and later a lending library to support the business. In all three businesses the families of the original founders carried the interests on well into the twentieth century. Other photographers from the Keswick area went off to take their own pictures to sell in their own shops instead of selling the mass of material being offered by the 'big three'.

Some of the pictures used are by photographers from further afield, for the Keswick holiday trade offered rich pickings. Where possible the photographer is named with the picture, but it is unfortunate that many pictures come to us, even from famous studios, with no identification and we can only guess at the source.

For readers interested in the Lake District area at the turn of the century, this book complements four others in the Britain in Old Photographs series published by Alan Sutton. South Westmorland Villages, The Westmorland Lakes, The Eden Valley, Westmorland and Kendal cover the old County of Westmorland, and Lancashire North of the Sands, written with my friend John Garbutt, offers an insight into an area that was part of Lancashire but belonged more to the Lakes.

My thanks must go to the early photographers whose work allows us to glimpse their times. Some pictures are of more recent vintage and illustrate things now lost. Even with protection by such as the National Trust, the Friends of the Lake District and the Lake District National Park the Keswick area has changed much in the last few decades. Why no one can devise road signs for use in fragile areas such as this to replace the metal tube and tin plate signs which everywhere ruin the outlook today is an enduring mystery.

I must thank in particular my friend Preston Whiteley who has been photographing the changing local railway scene for some years. He has most kindly let me use his unpublished pictures of the now lost Keswick railway, the closure of which must rank as one of the most shortsighted of a number of bad government policies affecting the area in recent times. The 'C, K & P' could have been a major tourist attraction instead of the ruin it is today. 'When the railway ran to Keswick', sang the 1970s bard of the difficulties of Lake District traffic problems, 'You could travel there by train.' The photographs in this book capture the area when access was being improved but traffic, in the main, was not a problem.

John Marsh
Spring 1993

One

Keswick and Derwentwater

The Keswick Hotel, the railway station and the growing town at the turn of the century are here photographed from Latrigg, giving almost a bird's-eye view of what is now a much changed scene. The railway was opened for passenger traffic in January 1865.

Keswick railway station in steam days, photographed by Preston Whiteley of Kendal, shows an Ivatt 'Mogul' class 2-6-0 on a westbound train on 27 July 1963. Both the C, K & P and the days of steam were nearly at an end.

'Keswick lads off to the front, 14 September 1914.' Volunteers into the 'Pals' battalions in Kitchener's army. Newspapers quoted rousing recruiting speeches, such as 'Mothers and wives are urged to give up your sons and husbands', and a poster from Lord Lonsdale had asked 'Are you a man or a mouse?' Canon Rawnsley penned a three verse ditty, 'Fare ye well Borderers', which ended, 'Forward to victory—victory and peace.' 'C' Company of the Fourth Btn, Territorial Force of the Border Regiment had its drill hall in Southey Street, and Captain Joseph Broatch VD (Solicitor and Clerk to the Magistrates) was the Captain.

Diesel units (the 6.55 to Penrith and the 6.42 to Workington) are waiting in both platforms at Keswick station on 27 July 1963 in this picture by Preston Whiteley. The DMUs were introduced on the line in 1955 in the hope of improved income. They worked the line through from Workington and Cockermouth to Penrith until April 1966 when the line from Cockermouth to Keswick was closed.

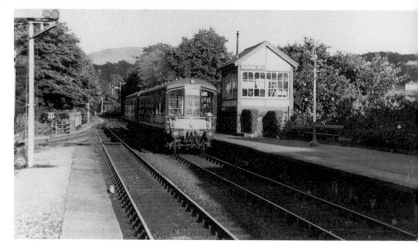

The signal box and the island platform on Keswick Station can be seen in these two pictures, by Preston Whiteley, in the last year of full working.

The Penrith to Workington DMU passes No. 1 signal box on 31 August 1965. A passenger service of sorts was to survive on the Penrith to Keswick section until March 1972, when Keswick station was finally closed. The shortsighted closure policy can only be regretted today.

The Keswick Hotel in the 1880s, seen across the land that was to become Fitz Park. In this photograph the hotel is only a few years old as is the railway station, standing to the left of the hotel. A room, breakfast and lunch at the Keswick were 2s. 6d. each. Dinner was 4s. 6d. and tea 1s. 6d.

Coaches off on their then daily trips stand at the front of the Keswick Hotel at the turn of the century. Pettitts called this picture '10 a.m. off for the day'. There were four 'famous' tours: 1. Borrowdale & Buttermere; 2. Round Thirlmere; 3. Round Bassenthwaite, and 4. Windermere. Glimpses of each will be seen in the following pages.

The smoking room at the Keswick Hotel, photographed by George Abraham. 'There are no two better Hotels in the Lake District than the Keswick & the Derwentwater,' said a London and North Western Railway guide of the times. 'The views to be seen from the grounds present a magnificent panorama of mountain line extending from fifty to sixty miles.'

The land between the railway station, adjoining the Keswick Hotel, and the river and town was laid out as the Fitz Park as a result of an idea by guide writer and Keswick railway station master Henry Irwen Jenkinson who, with Mr Fisher-Crosthwaite, sought the help of local gentry in the early 1880s to purchase the land and lay out a park. In this turn of the century Valentine of Dundee picture the tennis courts are in the centre.

Fitz Park photographed by R. Henderson of Station Street, Keswick, showing the bowling green with the tennis courts in the background. (The secretary of the Fitz Bowling Club was T. Lancaster.) Other facilities included a cycle track and cricket ground and a museum next to the Park Lodge.

Spectators view tennis in progress in Fitz Park around 1910 in a picture by Clark of Main Street. At the turn of the century W.W. Hindle of 22 Stanger Street was the secretary of the Keswick Lawn Tennis Club.

The war memorial had appeared on the corner of Station Road and Penrith Road when Abrahams pictured the scene as an AA man saluted a member's car. How many of those seen on page 11 have their names here? (See also page 19.)

Greta View Guest House, c. 1900, with a wagonette waiting for passengers. The high treats of a holiday in Keswick were the charabanc trips to the passes and lakes in the area. The Borrowdale, Honister and Buttermere 'round' offered the most excitement.

Shu-le-Crow Cottage on the Penrith Road had this rather dull picture taken by Pettitts as a postcard for their guests. The photographers offered all boarding houses pictures to sell to their guests.

The Oaks, Church Street used Henry Mayson to picture their boarding house. 'Apartments and board, central to all tours, cycle accommodation, boat for hire, bath' wrote proprietor Mrs Cutts on the side of the picture.

Sunny Bank, Chestnut Hill, photographed by Abrahams about 1920. This picture was used as a Christmas card in December 1921. Many people used a picture of their house as a greetings card, with some photographers offering seasonal holly, etc. to assist. (See page 110.)

Rigg's coach, pictured by Abrahams at the corner of Station Road and Penrith Road, setting off on the trip to Windermere. The war memorial seen on page 16 was yet to appear. The railway stations of Windermere and Keswick were connected by horse coaches for many decades, with Rigg's Royal Mail coaches being the last horse-drawn Royal Mail stage coaches in the country.

Station Road, with two Rigg's coaches, appeared on this 1905 W.H. Smiths 'Kingsway' series picture. Bell writes, on 13 August 1907 to Miss Sutcliffe in Manchester, a typical Keswick comment, ' I hope you are having good weather. I am sorry to say we are not.'

Station Street leading to Station Road, Keswick, by Henry Mayson. A local hotel charabanc passes Taylor's 'Lake District Coaches' booking office next to W.H. Smiths 'bookstall'.

Outside the Royal Oak Hotel soon after the First World War. Abrahams shows a traffic mix up which includes two motor cars, a hotel 'bus' and a charabanc (both on the wrong side of the road) as well as the Buttermere coach in the background.

Pedestrians in Station Street outside J. Telford's watch and clock makers shop include a very small delivery girl—cheap labour or helping in the family business?

The Royal Oak Hotel with its Garage, and Messenger's 'Lake District Coaches' booking office. Note the deck chairs facing the street. Had the car, registration number AO 117, broken down?

The lounge at the Royal Oak Hotel, photographed by Abrahams in the 1930s. It was a very modern room indeed at the time, with what looks to be 'Lloyd Loom' wicker furniture and electric lighting.

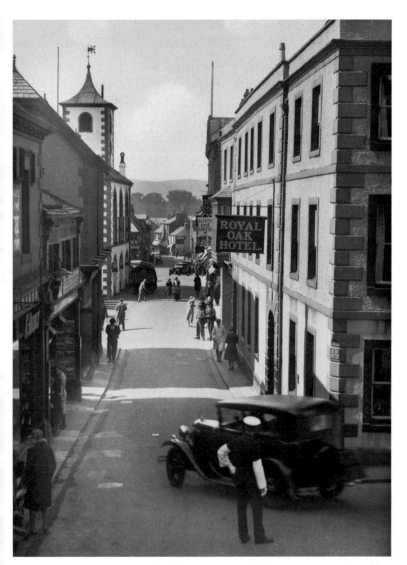

The point duty policeman on the Royal Oak corner in the 1930s. Every passing vehicle got his personal attention. The Cumberland and Westmorland Constabulary of the period was run by a 'joint committee' of both County Councils and all officers wore 'flat' caps with a white top piece in summer.

Market day in the Market Place, Keswick. This mid-nineteenth-century picture is by Alfred Pettitt, who had opened a photographic studio in Keswick in 1858 when he and his brother moved from Grasmere. When postcards came into use at the turn of the century the picture was reproduced in that medium. Note the Museum of Local Natural History in the Moot Hall. Mabel used the card in 1908 to wish her uncle, Mr Bywater, 'Many happy returns'.

The Market Place, c. 1900, by G. Abraham. In the background is John Morley's milliners and dressmaking business, next to Walker's Central Hotel, which also advertised as Rigg's Royal Mail Coach Office.

A busy Market Place on market day, c. 1900, by Henry Mayson. In the background can be seen the 'High class Ices and confections' cart of Italo Serefini, Confectioner and Pastry Cook from 45 Castlegate, Penrith. Farmers and smallholders sell fruit and vegetables while children play.

Keswick's main street was becoming a car park when Pettitt took this picture in the 1920s. The card carries the note, 'We have seen the tents of the Indian black people here for the Convention.' Motors and cycles are for hire at the Keswick Garage on the right. The Whitehaven Steam Laundry shop is on the left.

The same part of Main Street, c. 1900, by Stengal & Co. of London. The Queen's Hotel is on the left with two coaching ladders by the door and advertisements for coach trips. Rooms could be had from 2s., breakfast was 1s. 6d., lunch 2s. 6d. and tea 1s. Pension was 9s. 6d. per day or 55s. per week. There is not a car to be seen.

The Keswick Interdenominational Religious Convention was a source of much income to the town's photographers. Crowds were herded into one picture to increase possible sales. Here is a G.P. Abraham's Convention photograph from soon after the First World War.

During an earlier Convention the crowds are caught near the great tent and its associated small tents. Hymn books 'for Convention week' are for sale.

Valentine's of Dundee also considered it worthwhile to join the local photographers for Convention photograph sales. The great tent with the Convention bookstall advertised is pictured around 1905. Business in postcards and stamps reached an annual high during Convention week.

Inside the great tent at the 1910 Convention. 'We are having a great time here,' reads the postcard. 'I wish you and all my friends could be here. I have heard enough in these few days to last me the rest of my life. Tonight we are going to hear the Revd T.B. Mayer. We had a wonderful Jewish Missionary meeting yesterday—I never was at such a meeting.'

The 1913 Convention crowd outside the tent caught the attention of the Pettitts. The Scripture Gift Mission advertises on the left and the Jesus Missionary bookstall is on the right. The horrors of the First World War were just over a year away.

'The Arts and Sciences' tableau, prepared on a flat cart for the Keswick parade, about the time of the First World War. No doubt it drew its inspiration from the Arts and Crafts activities that, at the time, were an important part of Keswick life, inspired by the likes of Canon Rawnsley and Marion Twelves. The photograph is by Pettitts.

Inside Tom Wilson's Waverley Café, Keswick in the 1930s. The provision of 'café' refreshments had grown with the advent of day trippers by rail and motor coach. Lunch and tea, as well as snack refreshments, all with waitress service, were offered for a few shillings each.

The pencil works of Messrs Hogarth & Hayes at the turn of the century was, said Pearson's Gossipy Guide, 'like that of Messrs Banks & Co., always courteously open to the inspection of visitors who may buy, if they like, as a souvenir of their visit, a pencil as long as their arm.'

The Till family and their Rock Band photographed by Henry Mayson and reproduced on a carte-de-visite card in the late nineteenth century, decades before postcards came into use. It took eleven years for the Tills to collect 'Gneiss, Schist and Hornblende rocks of the perfect form', to make musical instruments much enjoyed by tourists and locals. By 1900 Messrs Abrahams had acquired the rocks and used them as part of their studio display, a 'Tour of Lakeland'.

The Museum and Art Gallery Building around 1902, photographed as part of the James Clark (of Main Street) series. Admission was 6d. and the display included the famous Joseph Flintoft relief map which, although the first, had a scale of only three inches to the mile, whereas both Mayson's and Abraham's, which were built much later, were six inches to the mile and based on the Ordnance Survey. The excitement gleaned from examination of the relief maps is hard to envisage today.

The Ruskin Linen Industry came to Keswick from Langdale when Canon and Mrs Rawnsley and their housekeeper Marion Twelves moved from Sawrey to Crosthwaite in 1883, bringing with them their great interest in folk art. Marion Twelves is spinning at the door of St George's Cottage. The Pepper family was left in charge of the St Martin's 'industry' in Langdale.

The Keswick School of Industrial Arts was founded by Canon and Mrs Rawnsley in 1884, 'for the promotion of a recreative and remunerative industry in Keswick'. Paley and Austin of Lancaster were called in to design and build a workshop and showroom which were completed in 1894. 'All who are interested in the revival of industrial arts for rural neighbourhoods should not fail to visit this school,' said one guide. Pettitt used the national photographer Frith's Saxony printer to reproduce these two pictures from around 1905 on to postcards with appropriate 'Arts and Crafts' style script.

Interior of Keswick School of Art.

The Heads must have caused many an ex-sailor to smile, but this name was given to a row of houses which originally looked out over pastures green at the Keswick end of Derwentwater. Road engineers in recent times have changed much of the foreground of both of these pictures by Maysons. In the earlier (top) view, from the turn of the century, horses graze before the park was constructed. In the latter, from the 1930s, the 'private enterprise' amusement park kiosk and shop have appeared but crops were harvested where now a modern road blights the scene.

The church of St John the Evangelist, c. 1902, by Valentine's of Dundee. Originally erected in 1838 as Keswick started to expand, the architect was Anthony Salvin (who had just completed Holy Trinity in Ulverston). The church, which 'exhibits all the vices of its period' according to Pearson's Guide from the turn of the century, was originally only a chapel for Crosthwaite but in 1856 it became the parish church for the town. Aisles were added in 1862 and 1882, and in 1889 the chancel was lengthened. A 1976 guide calls it 'a prominent landmark with its tall spire' and adds that the churchyard, where Sir Hugh Walpole is buried, is worth visiting if only for the fine views of Derwentwater. John Marshall, the Leeds manufacturer who paid £4,100 for the church's erection, must have hoped for a better reception for his fine church.

St John's Terrace, c. 1900. On 18 May 1911 S.B. Hawell wrote from No. 8 to Miss Deardon of Grange-over-Sands, 'The first house on the right is where I am located. A lovely view of St John's church and Causey Pike from our drawing room windows.'

The Greta near the bridge, c. 1910, by Abrahams. The Romantic movement guessed the name Greta originally meant 'The River of Singing Waters'. Here the river bank is occupied by part of the plumbago or wadd industry in the shape of the offices and works of Banks & Co's pencil works where Henry Birkbeck was the manager.

The Greta Bridge receives the attention of a lady artist at the turn of the century. The view from the same site today would lack the romance being caught on canvas by this lady. The addition of highways department pipe and sheet metal signs in our times has desecrated this bridge and Keswick.

'Greta Hall was home to Coleridge from 1800 to 1810 and of Southey from 1803 to 1843,' reads the writing on this picture by Pettitts. Pearson's Guide adds that it was 'here Coleridge became confirmed in the dreadful opium habit'. The poet Southey died here in 1843 after taking over the whole house in 1809. Pevsner made scant comment on the place, noting that 'the house looks later than the eighteenth century'.

Crosthwaite church of St Kentigern is on as ancient a Christian site as any in the county. This photograph of around 1905 is by Henry Mayson. The vicar at the time was Canon H.D. Rawnsley, a friend of Ruskin, the founder of the National Trust and chaplain to the 1st (Cumberland) Volunteer Battn of the Border Regiment based at the drill hall in Southey Street. One can but wonder if the farm workers collecting their turnips realized the importance of their vicar's many interests.

Abraham's view of Crosthwaite church from the road near the old school, c. 1905. The Reformation reached Crosthwaite in 1571 when it was realized the old 'popish' ways under the Ratcliffes had not been altered. A 'commission' from the Crown was sent to put things at the church in Elizabethan order. Even then, for the next 200 years, the Ratcliffe family did not change, but their devout persistence led to their downfall locally in the eighteenth century when they supported the Jacobite rebellion. Canon Rawnsley wrestled with this sorry tale for devout Christians in his writings for many years.

CROSTHWAITE CHURCH, KESWICK. 96935. J.V.

The interior of St Kentigern's church, c. 1905, by Valentine's of Dundee. It has obviously been altered over many centuries, with a major early Victorian 'restoration' under Sir Giles Scott taking place in 1845. Surprisingly, Pevsner, in his report on this important church, does not record this major restoration by so eminent a Victorian architect. The remains of the Ratcliffe family, the Derwentwaters, so important in the area until the Jacobite rebellion, when their faith found them on the wrong side, were removed from their family chapel inside the church and dumped in the churchyard in the frenzy of unchristian behaviour associated with those days after 1746. The two battered stone figures on display in the church today are believed to be members of the Ratcliffe family, but they say more about bigotry than about the Ratcliffes.

This picture of Causey Pike from Portinscale Bridge appeared in a London and North Western Railway guide of 1910. Cows standing in streams and lakes seemed to appeal to artistic photographers at the time. The realization of the smelly mess they caused must have come as a shock to many a city-dwelling Edwardian traveller; and the meaning of the name Portinscale as 'the prostitute's hut' was not advertised either.

Portinscale Bridge in around 1905, with the delivery cart of John Fisher 'confectioners and bakers' of 36 Station Street, Keswick, and its driver waiting on the bridge for Pettitt's photographer to take the picture. Did the Pettitts beg a ride for a tour of photo opportunities?

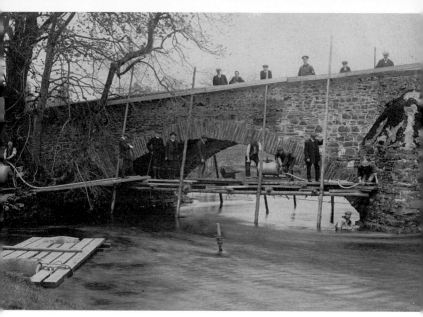

Portinscale Bridge was in such poor condition in 1907 that it was condemned. Canon Rawnsley was so taken aback by this that he organized opposition to the County Council, and had Mr Fox demonstrate his grouting procedures, used at Winchester Cathedral, on other local bridges. In 1911 the bridge was again condemned, and again the worthy Canon appealed with the result that, after a public enquiry, the grouting was carried out in 1912. Here a hand-driven compressor on the bank supports another on the planking, where a dog watches the work. Canon Rawnsley can be seen on the planks near the arch of the bridge.

Portinscale village in two pictures by Pettitts. At the turn of the century the population of 990 souls lived in 13,872 acres of land, with 881 acres of water. John Fleming Brownrigg of Milbeck Hall was Clerk to the Parish Council and Overseer of the Poor in 1910, while the McIntosh family ran the post office and shop as they had from the nineteenth century. John Hetherington Mitchinson was a farmer at Portinscale House in 1906 but had moved to 'The Mount', advertising apartments, before 1914. In the lower picture a delivery cart is outside Ivy and Rose Cottages. The scene is much changed today.

Pettitts pictured the awkward corner in Portinscale in the 1920s before the road engineers finally 'improved' things. From Portinscale House on the right to Ivy and Rose Cottages on the left a much changed scene today. Compare the road level with the view at the top of page 43.

The Derwentwater Hotel at Portinscale in the mid-nineteenth century when Mrs Anne Bell was the proprietor. The garden of the then nearly new establishment looks to be rather overgrown. Boats could be hired on the lake and the fare on the horse-drawn bus to and from Keswick Station was 6d. This hotel was reckoned by the guide book writers for the London and North Western Railway to be one of the two best hotels in the Lakes—the Keswick Hotel being the other.

Derwent Bank Holiday Fellowship Home, with long shorts much in evidence in this photograph by Maysons. The house, described in 1900 as a 'fine mansion and the home of W.J.P. Fawcus Esq.', was later occupied by Mrs Edmondson until the mid-1930s, when it was taken into use as a Fellowship Hostel and is now holiday flats.

Henry Mayson photographed a royal visit to Keswick in September 1902 when Princess Louise visited the town and opened the nearby Brandlehow Park for the National Trust. Here she is outside Mayson's Drapers in the town centre.

Brandlehow boat landing. Brandlehow Park was acquired by the National Trust in 1902.
A London and North Western Railway guide said, 'Visitors are free to enjoy its delights on
condition that they do no damage to plant life or tree life, but they are called on to help to hand
it on unspoiled by picnic papers and luncheon debris, unrobbed of its ferns and flowers, its bird
life, its beast life, to other seasons and to succeeding generations of lovers of natural beauty.'

Two views of the Lakeside Tea Gardens at the Keswick end of Derwentwater in the early 1930s. John Anthony Spedding of 'Storms', Penrith Road, Keswick formed the Storms Farm Dairy Ltd and ran both the Lakeside Tea Gardens and the Gowbarrow Tea House on Ullswater. He also had a café in the Market Square.

1033. VIEW FROM LAKE SIDE TEA GARDENS DERWENTWATER, KESWICK.

47

The Derwentwater boat landings as illustrated in the London and North Western Railway guide in 1910. The boat proprietors in those days were the Blacks, the Fishers, the Hodgsons, the Milburns, the Scotts and the Sparks as well as the partnership of Smith and Telford.

Valentine's of Dundee photographed the piers (numbered one to fourteen) at the boat landings about the time of the First World War, but the postcard was sent in 1930 to South Shields to say, 'We have done 200 miles by motor car to this place. Beautiful. I don't think I will ever forget it.'

The Lodore and Derwentwater Hotels' electric launch May Queen was powered by batteries which were said to be recharged by a generator driven by the Lodore Falls (which must have caused difficulties). This picture from around 1905 shows a crowded launch and pier but the postcard reads, 'It's charming, especially when one has it alone.'

The famous Friars Crag could not look more desolate than on this Rock Brothers of London picture from around 1910. Rock Brothers were guide book photographers and one wonders how attracted their clients were. 'Boats can be hired at the Friars Crag landing stage for 1s. an hour or 5s. a day,' said Pearson's Guide.

A more delightful view of Friars Crag was taken by Valentine's of Dundee before 1910. John Ruskin called the view one of the three loveliest in Europe, which brought millions to compare. Pearson's Gossipy Guide advises, 'Follow a broad and trampled path with a length of ugly railings on the right till the path ends abruptly on the edge of a marginal cliff where the view of Derwentwater is lovely in the extreme.' Messrs Carrs of Carlisle used the postcard as a visiting card for their biscuit representatives in 1910.

'A cattle scene' on Derwentwater by Abrahams was no doubt taken to satisfy the longing of holiday-makers for cows in water. Such 'artistic' views were taken all over the Lake District by all the photographers. Some photographers' cows might, of course, by photographic fakery, be found in Lakes other than the original. Below, Maysons caught a flock of the local Herdwick sheep near Lodore. Sheep breeding, centred on the Keswick November 'tup fair', improved the Herdwick breed through the nineteenth century but failed to eliminate the homing instinct which took sold Herdwicks back to their native 'heaf' (or home fell pasture), much to the annoyance of the new owner.

The Scotts' new Lodore Hotel in the late nineteenth century, possibly soon after completion but before it was extended to the left of the picture. Their bus met every train at Keswick station (fare 6d. each way). The entrance to the famous falls, for those not staying at the hotel, was through a wicker gate on the Borrowdale side of the hotel–price 3d. The poet Robert Southey complained at the cost of buying an English echo when he wrote of the price charged to hear the cannon used by the old Lodore Hotel.

The electric launch, the Lodore Hotel (with extensions) and the head of Derwentwater pictured by Pettitts, c. 1900. Rooms could be had at the Lodore Hotel for 2s. 6d., and breakfast was the same. Lunch was 2s., tea 1s. 6d. and dinner 4s. Pension was 9s. a day, or 63s. a week.

Lodore Falls in Summer.   Abraham's Humorous Series, Keswick.
No. 1 (copyright).

" How does the water come down at Lodore ? "
A dry-season Tourist once thought to explore,
But he failed to discover the famous cascade,
So enquired in despair of a Cumbrian maid ;
" Indeed, Sir," quoth she, with a toss of her bonnet,
Ye may well seek Lodore, for ye're sitting upon it ! "

Abraham's series of humorous postcards included this, with its verse about the Lodore Falls
and their not infrequent lack of water. Pearson's Guide warned, 'Man, of course, has, as
usual, done his best to disfigure, and degrade and destroy it. . . . The paths are trampled in all
directions and the rocks scratched and polished by the feet of myriads of tourists.' Times have
not changed in this respect.

Lodore Falls without water and with tourists, around 1902, confirms the problem. Southey's jingle about 'spreading and threading, whizzing and hissing, dripping and skipping, whitening and brightening, dividing and gliding and sliding, grumbling, rumbling and tumbling, delaying and straying, playing and spraying, advancing and prancing and glancing and dancing and so never ending, but always descending–and this way does the water come down at Lodore', must have been rather hard for these visitors to believe. 'At all times', said Pearson's Guide, 'we imagine the tourist will be gratified with the prospect of the chaos of tumbled rocks, the beetling cliffs and the waving foliage.'

Lodore Falls, (Frozen) 173
Mayson

Maysons caught the Falls frozen solid in the 1920s. Photographers competed with each other for different angles to sell their postcards. Frozen lakes and waterfalls helped.

Above Lodore the Ashness Bridge also attracted many photographers both local and national. Here are two views by national photographers. The top is of a girl on a tumble-down bridge and is from the turn-of-the-century Pearson's Guide. The bottom view, with even more of the bridge parapet missing, is by Rock Brothers of London for the London and North Western Railway guide. Thousands were drawn by guide books to this view. It was possible to include Friars Crag, a boat trip on the lake and a walk to Ashness and Lodore on one of the 'Day in the Lakes' railway trips to Keswick.

Two

Borrowdale to Crummock

23.

High Lodore, Borrowdale.

High Lodore Farm, Borrowdale, c. 1905, by H. Henderson of Station Street, Keswick. Mrs June Wilson was the farmer and Mr Wilkinson Magee the blacksmith. 'Overleaf is our house,' read the card posted in August 1909, 'lovely in every way, view, food, comfort, my word you should be here and then you both need no more of this world.'

BORROWDALE, FROM HIGH LODORE. 2054.

Looking over High Lodore Farm towards the Borrowdale Hotel, Troutdale and the jaws of Borrowdale by Pettitts, before the First World War. The modern view comes as a shock in what appears to be an unchanging scene.

The Keswick to Seatoller bus—a Daimler coach, registration number AO 9916—ploughing through the flood waters. The Cumberland Motor Services set up their offices in Main Street, Keswick in the mid-1920s and, along with other proprietors, built a bus station and garage very soon afterwards, which served the town for about sixty years.

Grange-in-Borrowdale photographed by Stengal of London, c. 1900. Pearson's Guide says, 'A quiet little hamlet (no Inn).' The name derives from the days when the Cistercian monks of Furness Abbey had a grange here as part of their extensive wool trade interests. The locals in times gone by acquired the derogatory nickname of 'Gowks'. Was it the lead mining or the inbreeding?

Henry Mayson took up a position near the double bridges shown above to capture Grange around 1905. This bridge was regrouted by Mr Ford as part of Canon Rawnsley's efforts to save Portinscale Bridge in the early years of the twentieth century (see page 42).

Brittain and Wright of Stockton-on-Tees captured this view of visitors arriving at Manor House, Grange-in-Borrowdale, around 1905. George Mounsey advertised as joiner and builder, with apartments to let, while Mrs Mounsey ran the post office at the turn of the century.

Mrs Zonassi's House, Grange was photographed by Henry Mayson so that Mrs Jane Zonassi could sell the cards o her visitors. In 1906 Charles Frederick Zonassi advertised 'apartments' at Bleak House, Grange. By 1910 Jane Zonassi was advertising rooms. Fom 1921 to 1925 she advertised fom Bella Vista.

Bowder Stone Cottage, photographed by Henry Mayson, advertising teas and rock. William Weightman, who was also the road foreman, ran the Bowder Stone house in 1900. A much earlier owner, James Pocklington, anxious to attract tourists, had a hole drilled under the stone and employed an old lady who charged visitors a small fee to shake hands with her through the hole, to improve their luck.

The Bowder Stone photographed in the 1860s by Alfred Pettitt and reproduced on to the carte-de-visite type picture which predated picture postcards by forty years. The Victorian advertisement offered, 'an immense mass of basaltic or porphyritic green-stone rock, 62 feet in length, 36 feet in perpendicular height, 89 feet in circumference and contains 23,090 cubic feet, weighs 1,971 tons 13 cwts.'

The Bowder Stone in the 1920s as photographed by Edward Sankey, the brilliant photographer from Barrow in Furness. Masters of their craft, the Sankeys, father Edward and son Kenneth, must rank among the highest for picture content and quality of reproduction. Their usual haunts were in Furness but they photographed locations further afield when required. (See also page 63.)

Watendlath Farm photographed by Henry Mayson as the sheep were being gathered in. John Wilson, a farmer like his father before him, offered apartments to subsidize his farming. This photograph was probably commissioned to encourage visitors.

'The Home of Judith Paris' is the title of this view of Watendlath by Henry Mayson. Author Hugh Walpole improved the Watendlath tourist prospects following the publication of his Herries novels, with their Lakeland location. They added to the romance offered to visitors to the Lake District by such as Beatrix Potter and Arthur Ransome.

Watendlath Tarn by Henry Mayson. Here two ancient wool trade packhorse routes, one from Wythburn and one from Armboth, join to connect Thirlmere with Keswick. Today the area is poised for the next television production of Walpole's stories, a poor alternative to the hill farming subsidy many would prefer, but an unfortunate reality as the true Lake District is displaced by the idealistic falseness of tourism publicity.

Low Farm, Watendlath in the 1920s, again by Sankeys of Barrow. The Richardson family offered teas and milk for sale. The car in the background was probably Sankey's, as it carries the Barrow registration number EO 3286.

Henry Mayson photographed his friend, the local eccentric Millican Dalton, on High Lodore with ice axe and rope in mid-summer to produce a postcard for Dalton to sign for his admirers. Having left his career in insurance in London, Dalton called himself the 'Professor of Adventure' and lived in the wilds of Lakeland, often in a cave.

The Borrowdale Birches were much photographed by the rival photographers. Henry Mayson's view catches the Borrowdale carrier with his cart pulled by a white horse. Thomas Bragg, of Yew Tree House, Stonethwaite, and Thomas Graham of Castle Lodge, Rosthwaite were listed in local directories at the turn of the century as carters, while Thomas Graham of the Pack Horse, Keswick advertised as carrier into Borrowdale each Saturday.

A 'Seatoller, Grange and Keswick' charabanc coach in the days before motorized transport. The Lodore, Borrowdale and Royal Oak Hotels each had charabancs or buses which met trains and the Rigg's Mail coaches from Windermere. Standard fare seems to have been 6d.

BORROWDALE.

Borrowdale in the snow. Henry Mayson must be given top marks for taking the opportunity to increase sales. The Herdwick sheep look surprised to find themselves being photographed instead of being fed.

The road into Rosthwaite pictured by Henry Mayson. Is this the same carrier as on page 67, with his white horse but this time with a covered carriage? Note the unmade, rutted, track-like road; and also that the telephone had arrived.

Ernest Plaskett was the bootmaker whose shop can be seen on the left of this view of Rosthwaite by Pettitts just before the First World War. The boot shop was run by Edward Coward in around 1900.

'In Rosthwaite' by G.P. Abraham shows the Royal Oak Hotel on the right, with an unmade road. In 1910 Thomas Hawkrigg advertised the Royal Oak as a temperance hotel, apparently suggesting a requirement for unlicensed accommodation.

'Rigg's Royal Oak Hotel, Keswick' was the title of this postcard by Henry Mayson, from around 1905. This must have caused some confusion as the Royal Oak at Rosthwaite is shown (see pages 22 and 23). Tom C . Stanley was then the victualler at both the Royal Oak and the Scawfell Hotel. Breakfast cost 1s. 3d., lunch 2s., tea 1s. 6d. and dinner from 2s. 6d. to 3s.

The Scawfell Hotel, Rosthwaite photographed by Abrahams some years later when Samuel William Badrock was the proprietor. The open back car has the registration number B 4425.

During the years after the First World War a very common sight on the road from Honister quarries to Keswick station was the Foden six-ton steam wagon 'Mountaineer', registration number TU 2013, with Mr Hodgson its driver. The Buttermere Green Slate Quarry Company used it to transport loads to the station.

Rosthwaite, by Maysons (using the initials M.K.), shows a little girl from about the time of the First World War. The Revd John Thomas Ashworth lived at the vicarage and Mrs Elizabeth Bird was postmistress at the time. While the valley is famed for its 'wild' countryside, it still comes as a surprise to read that Mrs Annie Clyno was then listed as 'the missionary' at the Rosthwaite Unsectarian Mission!

On Friday 18 August 1922 a party of Norwegian scouts, the guests of J. Mortimer Sladen and his Windermere sea scouts, who were camping at Fell Foot, trekked over Stake Pass with members of the Windermere troop. Above they are seen at Rosthwaite before 'settling into the Borrowdale Institute' where they gave an impromptu concert the following evening and raised over £21 for the Institute funds. The concert was crowded and prompted Mr Sladen to remark: 'We should have charged five shillings to get in and ten shillings to get out again.' The trek support vehicle— Mr Sladen's car and trailer—is seen below en route.

Stonethwaite and Eagle Crag, in the early years of the century, by Abrahams. Fletcher Wren and Mrs Elizabeth Plaskett (is it her in the picture?) were listed as farmers, and Thomas Bragg as farmer and carter at Yew Tree House.

Stonethwaite, c. 1910, by Pettitts. Catching the delivery cart at the farm door. John Fleming, who was shown as road contractor, later became the sexton.

'Ring a roses' in Seatoller by Maysons, a dog looking on with great interest. The Jopson family offered apartments as well as being farmers. Isabella Pepper also advertised apartments at Seatoller House at the turn of the century.

Seatoller by Maysons from a field, a twisted tree apparently being of the greatest interest. Most of Seatoller was built by the Honister Quarry Company, as housing for its workers.

SEATOLLER. LAKE DISTRICT.

Seatoller was also visited by Aero Pictorial of Regent Street, London, this time with their photographer's feet firmly on the ground. The tree pictured appears on page 75.

The Lake Hotel, Keswick charabanc photographed at Seatoller, by Maysons. Guests at the hotel were enjoying one of the many coach trips that local hotels offered in competition with the coaching firms.

Seathwaite in Borrowdale, again by Aero Pictorial of London, who apparently wished to join in the huge postcard sales enjoyed by the local photographers. Two farm carts and a sled (or sledge) can be seen against the wall. Until the nineteenth century wheeled carts were virtually unknown in Borrowdale.

The base of Styhead pass, c. 1900, by Atkinsons of Ulverston. The demand for this type of photograph by holiday-makers to the Ulverston area demonstrates the popularity of the fells by the turn of the century.

Stockley Bridge and Styhead photographed by Alfred Pettitt, with a horseman negotiating the rough track. Many hotels advertised mountain ponies and guides to take visitors over passes such as this.

Stockley Bridge over Grains Gill Beck by Henry Mayson, including a horse and sledge (or sled). Wheelless carts had been used by local farmers from antiquity to bring bracken, injured sheep and stone from the fells to the farms.

Sheep gatherings on the high fells photographed by Henry Mayson, c. 1900. Grains Gill between Hind Side and Seathwaite Fell is seen in the top picture while, below, the shepherds and sheep are pictured at Styhead Tarn. The Borrowdale 'wadd' (or black lead) was used for sheep marking until the late 1800s. The first shepherds' guide to sheep wool and ear markings ('t'smit book') for this area was published by W. Stephen of Penrith around 1818.

ARROW HEAD, Gt GABLE   924

The Maysons also took themselves on to adjoining Great Gable to photograph the climbers on the favourite rock climbs. Here the party is seen on Arrow Head route. This was in direct competition with the Abrahams, who claimed to be *the* mountain photographers.

Wasdale Head chapelry 'is 7,000 acres, population in 1891 was 75 persons and the farmers are chiefly engaged in sheep farming'. At the turn of the century the Wilsons owned the Temperance Hotel, Row Head, High Burnthwaite and Middle Row. Seen here in 1910 is John Wilson's Herdwick ram 'Samson', which was that year's champion tup.

Wasdale Head chapel interior, c. 1910, by W.H. Smiths. This tiny church, lit by oil lamps, was said to be the smallest chapel in England, at 40 by 17 feet. The site, according to Pearson's Guide, was 'the perfection of desolation without being, in any sense, dreary or uninviting'.

On Styhead Pass Pettitts photographed the horse transport of the day on the narrow track between Borrowdale and Wasdale. There are many romantic yarns about the smugglers who used this 'back door' from the coast to bring in liquor. Lanty Slee is reported to have used loads of the red 'rud', used to mark the tup at mating time and which he mined in Langdale, to hide his illicit 'udder stuff'.

The Borrowdale Valley from Great End

Borrowdale from Great End with Maysons back among the climbers. Sprinkling Tarn and Sprinkling Crags point the way to Derwentwater and Keswick.

North View from Glaramara was another of Mayson's grand panoramas from the centre of the mountains, offering visitors postcards in obvious competition with the Abrahams.

'The last ascent of Scawfell Pike' by Abrahams shows the highest point of England and the track from Great End. This picture was printed in Sweden but, as with many other Abraham pictures, the reproduction was unfortunately of poor quality.

Summit of Scawfell Pike, E.L.D.   18

The summit of Scawfell Pike, c. 1905, by Brittain and Wright of Stockton-on-Tees in their 'Phoenix' photo series. They could get no higher in England than this—so here they came. This mountain was later given to the National Trust as a memorial to those who lost their lives in the First World War.

Scawfell. Pinnacle Arete.

Rock climbing photography became very popular, and here Atkinson and Pollitt of the Westmorland Gazette, Kendal pictured Scawfell pinnacle in the early 1930s. This mimics Pettitt, Abraham and Mayson in style—but the camera was much easier to carry by 1930.

The start of Honister Pass at Seatoller, Borrowdale, pictured by Abrahams in the 1930s with what looks like a Morris car (registration number RM 9167) commencing the climb. Bottom gear was needed all the way and overheating was not unlikely.

The refreshments hut on top of Honister in the 1930s. The deckchair and lots of liquid refreshments seem to indicate a warm summer's day, at a time when most people walked over from Borrowdale to Buttermere.

The incline railway of the Buttermere Green Slate Quarry Co. on Honister was built to take stone from Dubs Quarry to the slate company workshops on Honister Hause. There was a drum winding house at the top. 'The path between the quarry buildings and Dubs Quarry is the straightest mile in England,' reported fell guide writer Alfred Wainwright in 1966, explaining that since the tracks were removed the route had become a walkers' path. It would seem it was also a path before.

Coaches descending Honister, c. 1900, by Henry Mayson. The ruts in the track are caused by the coaches descending with their brakes on; their wheels were chained and 'skidded' so that the horses pulled down hill as well as up.

The steep summit of Honister Pass by Pettitts, c. 1900. The ruts in the rough surface are more obvious. A slightly untrue camera angle suggests a steeper track. The road was not improved until 1934.

HONISTER PASS.

Mayson

Henry Mayson got nine charabanc coaches into this view of the top of Honister but, unfortunately, in climbing the fell to get the picture he also included the roof tops of the slate quarry buildings in the background. This was one of the most famous of the coaching 'rounds' from Keswick, offering two spectacular passes, the other being into Newlands from Buttermere.

Hassness, Buttermere by Maysons, c. 1910. Pearson's Guide told its readers that 'Buttermere is graced by a single habitation, the beautiful house of Hassness whose scattered plantations strike a welcome note of change in the otherwise universally prevailing wilderness.' Hassness, long the home of Mrs Reed, had become the Ghyll Retreat 'Home for Inebriates', run by Dr J.W. Cooper, when this picture was taken.

The Fish Hotel, Buttermere, again by Henry Mayson. In the early decades of this century James Edmondson offered Victualling and Posting at both the Buttermere and Fish Hotels. 'Post horses, mountain ponies and trustworthy guides' as well as many coach excursions were offered. Rooms cost from 2s. to 4s., breakfast 1s., lunch 2s., tea 1s. and dinner 2s. 6d. at both hotels.

Syke House received attention from both Mayson and Pettitt. The top picture shows Henry Mayson's turn of the century view when Robert Jackson, farmer, offered apartments. The later picture, again by Pettitts for Robert Jackson, shows the table laid with a tablecloth, and roses round the door. Visitors, it was hoped, would buy a postcard with their tea.

1 SYKE HOUSE. BUTTERMERE.

'Gathering the Fell sheep' by G.P. Abraham shows a shepherd and his dog and a couple of dozen sheep on the lower pastures where working sheep was much easier than on the high fells (see page 80). 'Laking wit' gimmer hogs', would probably be how the farmer would have described this gathering of Herdwick sheep for Mr Abraham's lens.

A charabanc leaving Buttermere, c. 1905, by Brittain and Wright. 'Buttermere village seems chiefly to consist of three small hotels and a smaller church,' said Pearson's Guide. 'The church, alas, has been rebuilt!' The sad tale of Mary Robinson, 'the maid (or beauty) of Buttermere', who was exploited by a scoundrel, drew many visitors. She is still being exploited today!

Solitude on Crummock was pictured by many of the competing photographers. This one is by Pettitts. Gina wished Miss F. Snaith of High Street, Wigton were here, according to the message on the back.

Hause Point at Crummock (misnamed House Point by the photographer, Walter Scott of Bradford, and Horse Point by others), showing a recently restored wall and a farm cart in the 1930s. 'The best general views of the lake can be obtained from this rocky point', said Bulmer's Guide.

SCALE FORCE, 52.
MAYSON, KESWICK.

Scale Force on Scale Beck off Starling Dodd is reputed to be the highest waterfall in the Lake District, for which reason, no doubt, Henry Mayson added its beauty to his range of postcards at the turn of the century. 'The water descends perpendicularly for 160 feet in a long silver column in a black and narrow synetic cleft, but the stream which feeds it is very short and the volume can only be called considerable after copious rain,' said Pearson's Guide.

Loweswater, c. 1905. 'We may be going there at Whitsuntide,' says Maggie Coffie to Philip on 7 February 1907. 'If we do, Betty promises we shall be taken to the same spot—an inducement to go to anyone who knows how disastrous snap shots sometimes are.'

Loweswater and Mellbreak by G.P. Abraham just after the First World War, with cows in a field. They are very different from those found in the district today. It was reported that the only two adjacent buildings in the parish were the Kirkstiles Inn and the church of St Bartholomew.

'Under Mellbreak', by Maysons. The unmade road and tumble-down buildings point to the problems of the years between the wars when the great depression hit the West Cumberland area.

BUTTERMERE HAWSE 59

Richardson Henderson, bookseller of 25 Station Street, Keswick, wanted nothing from the competing photographers, preferring to go out in his trap to take his own pictures. Here, from around 1905, is his view which he called Buttermere Hause (which should have been Newlands Hause—see next page) which was reproduced on to postcards. 'This is part of the road we were on yesterday,' wrote 'H', who stayed at the Belevedere, Keswick in August 1908. 'Pretty wild isn't it?'

57. MOTORING IN LAKELAND. CLIMBING BUTTERMERE HAUSE.

Buttermere Hause—or should it be Newlands Hause—with open touring car, registration number OM 1873, photographed by Abrahams in the 1920s. Buttermere Hause is on Hause Point at the lakeside on Crummock Water if the Ordnance Survey is to be believed—which is possibly doubtful as their surveyors renamed many places.

Three

Newlands, Bassenthwaite and Skiddaw

363 The Devils Elbow.

'The Devils Elbow with Coaches returning from Buttermere' is the lengthy title of this photograph by Pettitts. Brakes hard on, ruts in the road caused by the braked wheels, and some of the party walking down are all typical of coaching over the Lakeland passes. 'There are three exceedingly dangerous corners, one of them without a C.T.C. warning board—the road is also infested with gates,' said Pearson's Gossipy Guide.

"A Lakeland Shepherd" 833

The title 'A Lakeland Shepherd' was shared by Mayson and Abraham for these two pictures for tourists. Henry Mayson caught a lamb being brought down by a shepherd but George Abraham added the glorious pun 'The Cast Shoe' (or should it be cast ewe?) as a subtitle to his picture. Many injured sheep were brought down for butchering—a fact that few tourists would care to be made aware of. Note that horses were used without a saddle.

497. "THE CAST SHOE"
A LAKELAND SHEPHERD
(ABRAHAMS SERIES)

The Blencathra pack hunting in Newlands in the 1920s, pictured by Maysons. Fox hunting was carried out on a regular basis to keep down the fox population. Foxes were (and are) a curse to hill farmers. For many years the Blencathra Pack had a very famous master, James William Lowther (see page 138).

'The Vale of Newlands' is the title Pettitts gave to this delightful picture from the turn of the century. In 1900, 108 people shared 1,160 acres. Twenty pupils were taught at the tiny school where the mistress was Jane Foster, who lived at Little Town. The postmaster at Stair was Nathan Robinson and the Revd B.L. Carr was the vicar.

In this picture of Stair village and Causey Pike, Abrahams seems also to have caught a road race with motor cycles, as a watching crowd can be seen on the right. What the man with gun and dog was doing in the middle of the road is difficult to guess! A sign offers 'Table water for sale'.

Newlands Hotel by Henry Mayson. The signs above the door show that it provided accommodation for the Cyclist Touring Club and was by then a temperance hotel. In the first decade of this century George Bird held the licence for the hotel and offered full pension for 5s. per day or 30s. per week.

Little Town in Newlands also by Mayson. Thomas Swainson and Joseph Wren both farmed there in 1910.

Newlands church, also by Mayson. Newlands became a parish in 1868. The church was rebuilt in 1843 and restored in 1885. Benjamin Lund Carr MA was vicar here from 1894 to 1913. George Bowe of Swinside, Portinscale was the parish clerk at the end of that time.

The Vale of Newlands with the church in the background. Near here the famous Goldscope copper mine also produced gold in the days of Queen Elizabeth I. Note the thatched hay stack in the field. John Foster Stewart became the vicar of this rural community in 1913.

'Near Mill Dam in Newlands' is the title of this picture by the Maysons, who seem to have photographed almost every corner of this valley in the first few decades of this century.

The Holiday Fellowship Newlands Guest House was opened at Stair just before the First World War. Maysons caught the scene in the early years.

The common room at the Newlands Guest House just after the First World War, in the Holiday Fellowship series of postcards taken to sell to the many holiday-makers in the fellowship who stayed at the house. The piano was the centre of the entertainment.

Two more photographs in the Holiday Fellowship series from just after the First World War show, above, an outdoor 'sing song' and, below, a highly 'posed' party climbing Causey. The growing demand for outdoor 'healthy' holidays for workers and managers was being catered for—fellowship being fostered by the shared experiences.

Braithwaite village, c. 1900, by the Pictorial Stationery Co. of London in their 'Peacock' series of 'Platino photos'. Frederick J. Farrer's grocery shop is on the left. He was also the Overseer for the Poor. The Puddle and Duck Street are names in this village which was once a working community of miners, farmers and workers in Wilson & Co.'s pencil works.

This picture of High Bridge, Braithwaite was used as a Christmas card in the early years of this century by Annie Bowe of Mossgarth, Braithwaite, where John Bowe was the farmer. 'Have a very happy Christmas, all join me in good wishes,' it read.

Little Braithwaite and the bridge across the Newland Beck, by Pettitts. Mrs L. Lodor offered apartments and William Fleming was the farmer at Little Braithwaite at the turn of the century.

Low Bridge at Braithwaite is in the centre of the village. This picture from around the time of the First World War by Maysons shows the unmade road through the village at that time.

Braithwaite station in two photographs from 27 July 1963 by Preston Whiteley. The neat station buildings and gardens can be seen in the top picture and, below, the 2.55 p.m. Penrith to Workington train is seen at the platform with one of the railway 'camping' coaches in the siding behind the platform. A comparison of these views of a delightful rural station with today is an indictment of the post-war 'planning' system and the shortsightedness of the county and national highways authorities in an area of great natural beauty.

Whinlatter Pass in the 1930s by Abrahams, with a solitary car on the right hand side of the unmade road. The Forestry Commission were changing the scene in these parts in spite of much criticism, of which, like the Manchester water engineers (see Thirlmere later) and the road engineers, they took no notice at all.

Braithwaite, Thornthwaite and Bassenthwaite from higher pastures by Henry Mayson. The limited plantations of trees in the early years of the twentieth century are in stark contrast to the later widespread coverage. Planting Thornwaite Forest began in 1920, and by 1950 had covered 3,485 acres.

The Bassenthwaite boat landings near the railway station were very popular with the visitors who came to the west end of the lake by train. 'Boats may be hired at the Pheasant Inn,' said the guides.

The now lost Bassenthwaite Lake station acted as post office for the parish of Wythop at the turn of the century. Two different visits by Preston Whiteley show (above) the view from the train as the DMU approached the station on 27 July 1963 and (below) the station platform with crossing gates closed on 16 April 1966. The gates were to remain closed until their removal, when the line was finally closed, only two days later. Compare the neatness of the railway days to today's ruination and untidiness.

Embleton station was the next on the line to Cockermouth and is here seen, also with its crossing gates closed, on 16 April 1966, photographed by Preston Whiteley. The platform was already overgrown. The shortsighted closure of the Cockermouth to Keswick line was two days away, and has been regretted by many ever since.

Ye Pheasant Inn, Bassenthwaite Lake should perhaps have been called the Station Inn, Piel Wyke, Wythop. This photograph was taken by Henry Mayson at the turn of the century. Lillian used the picture to tell Miss Ellwood of Mayo Street, Cockermouth that she was having 'a ripping time'.

The railway resulted in the development of boarding houses in the area then called Bassenthwaite Lake. This Henry Mayson picture was used by the Nelsons who stayed at Meadow Bank, 'the house on the right of picture', in July 1910. 'We have had bad wet weather but it has improved today,' said the message, so typical of a Lakeland holiday.

The Castle Inn, Bassenthwaite, c. 1905, by G.F. Stengal & Co. of London. Mrs Grace Watson was both victualler and farmer at the Castle Inn when the picture was taken. The Keswick coach 'round', costing 3s. per head, came as far as here before turning towards Piel Wyke.

The village green, Bassenthwaite, c. 1910, by Maysons. The Revd George Kenworthy MA was vicar and John Bowman of Halls was the local joiner and 'correspondent to the council school managers'. Jonathan Dixon of Vale View was the blacksmith and 'assistant overseer and clerk to the parish council'.

Bassenthwaite post office at the turn of the century, when Miss Mary Sproat (is that her in the picture?), was postmistress. 'Letters arrive 9.30 a.m. via Keswick, and despatched 3.15 p.m. No delivery or despatch on Sundays.' Bassenthwaite Lake post office at the railway station was really Wythop post office. The postmaster was the station master Thomas Allinson. Letters came from Cockermouth and there was a Sunday post dispatch at 6 p.m.

Uldale is hardly the venue for lovers that this Edwardian card, by B.B. of London from around 1905, would seem to suggest, although modern writers have recreated the myth for the area generally. Writing from the Uldale Schoolhouse on 11 August 1908, Jane tells Ethel Sayers of Rose Cottage, Broughton Moor that 'I am enjoying myself very much. It is raining this morning so I can not go out.'

Uldale and the church, which was erected in 1868/9, pictured by G.P. Abraham's, c. 1915. The church, which replaced an ancient church on the road to Ireby, was paid for by the Revd Jonathan Cape of Croydon in memory of his father, who was rector here for forty-four years. The Revd Jonathan Cape and his sister also endowed nearly £1,500 to the grammar school.

St Bridget's (or St Bega) church, Bassenthwaite is as ancient as any in the county and 'is sited in a beautiful isolated position by the lake of Bassenthwaite'. 'It was restored and almost entirely rebuilt in 1874' by the Spedding family of Mirehouse. Only odd bits of the original twelfth- and thirteenth-century church were left for our age to discover.

Armathwaite Hall, Bassenthwaite was built in 1881 by the architect Charles J. Ferguson of English Street, Carlisle. For many years it was occupied by the Hartley family but is here pictured as a hotel. Both pictures are from the 1930s and are by Abrahams. The wicker furniture in the ballroom was typical of the time (see page 22).

The Ball Room
Armathwaite Hall Hotel

Croft House, Applethwaite stands isolated on the road into the hamlet and offers a magnificent view of the central fells. Falder Green offered apartments here from around 1900 to the 1920s—is it his family in the picture?

Sunnyside, Applethwaite, with Elder Cottage behind and a milk maid and customer, was a colour postcard printed by James Clark of Main Street, Keswick around 1905. The picture was used as a Christmas card on 23 December 1908. The post office was run by Matthew Brandon—'deliveries from Keswick by footpost 8.45 a.m., despatch 4.45 p.m.' The Brandons, Matthew and Margery, had followed John Stamper of Millbeck in running Applethwaite post office.

Scar House, Applethwaite, c. 1900, photographed by W.H. Smiths in their 'Kingsway' series. W.H. Smiths had a shop in Station Street and a stall on the railway station at Keswick.

The London and North Western Railway considered cows were again appropriate when they photographed Applethwaite for the readers of their guide. By way of attracting visitors they added that Wordsworth almost came to live near here in 1803.

Maysons of Keswick produced this delightful view of a springtime shepherd with a small flock of five Herdwick ewes and five lambs returning to the 'heaf' (or home fell pasture) on the slopes of Skiddaw. The shepherd has a sheep dog, and a young dog learning the trade.

'The breast of Skiddaw and the hut' was the title given by J. Clark of Main Street, Keswick to his view of the popular way to the summit of the mountain. More Herdwick sheep, this time after clipping, seem an appropriate part of the view.

Further along the path, the Hawell Monument was photographed by Pettitts. Erected through the efforts of Canon Rawnsley to the shepherds of nearby Lonscale, Rawnsley penned, 'Great shepherd of thy heavenly flock, These men have left our hill, Their feet were on the living rock, Oh guide and bless them still.' Robert Walker Hawell farmed Lonscale farm at the turn of the century. Today's planning system, which brought the A66 nearby, would probably not permit the erection of such a monument. (See page 135.)

The Keswick Hut was on the way to the summit of Skiddaw and was visited by thousands of visitors each year. Pettitts photographed the scene about the time of the First World War. 'You would never think that I had some lemonade in the shop up Skiddaw', says the post card. The two refreshments huts are 'generally, though not invariably, open' said a guide.

The Blencathra Sanatorium was built in 1904 by the 'Cumberland branch of the National Association for the Prevention of Consumption and other forms of Tuberculosis' to house thirty patients. The top picture is by Brittain and Wright and shows the pavilions used for 'fresh air' treatment in the early years. The lower picture, by G.P. Abraham in 1915, shows one of the morale boosting events frequently held. Patients of both sexes and all ages are wearing fancy dress, with a group of nurses in their uniform in the centre. Antibiotics which were developed in the 1940s caused the closure of hospitals such as this, but were still a long way off in 1915.

Four

Threlkeld, Dockray, St John's and Thirlmere

The toll house on the road to Windermere, with a charabanc coach posed at the
Windebrowe junction, around 1905 by Alfred Pettitt. The trip to Ambleside via Thirlmere,
Dunmail and Grasmere was one of the regular holiday trips.

The Derwent Camp, c. 1905, photographed by Alfred Pettitt. Neat rows of military-type bell tents were hired out, offering cheap holidays to individuals or groups, often the latter, with lots of fresh air. Many adult groups such as St John's Ambulance, church fellowships and the like offered annual holidays to their members in camps such as this.

Three years before the outbreak of the Second World War this picture was taken on the Ambleside Road. 'September 1936' is written on the back of the picture which shows a plus-foured and rucksacked tourist in a raincoat apparently looking for a lift, while the grass verge is being raked clean. The only house then to be seen was the old tollbar cottage in the distance.

Castlerigg stone circle is one of the finest stone circles in the country and its location must be the most dramatic. Two of Henry Mayson's views from the turn of the century show the circle (top) looking east and (bottom) looking north towards Blencathra. Visitors wishing to view the circle were advised by guide books of the time to 'Take the train to Threlkeld and walk back.'

DRUIDS CIRCLE & SADDLEBACK

Scales Tarn by Henry Mayson, c. 1900, showing Sharp Edge in the background. The tarn is alleged to be so dark that tourists could come here and see 'the stars, while noon tide lights the sky' advised Sir Walter Scott.

SHARP EDGE SADDLEBACK
518

Sharp Edge from the top of Saddleback (or Blencathra), also by Henry Mayson, c. 1900. 'Negotiation needs care—it is considered rather formidable,' said a guide book. In the background is the Eden Valley area of north Westmorland. This was Alfred Wainwright's favourite route to the top of Blencathra.

A group of Herdwick rams in Threlkeld main street just after the First World War, photographed by Pettitts. The sign in the background, against the 1901 Public Rooms, says 'Danger, drive 5 miles per hour through the village.' The war memorial was later to appear on the left to remember the thirteen men killed in the First World War with, later, five more names for the Second World War.

Threlkeld church of St Mary, again photographed by Pettitts, was completely rebuilt in 1777. The Revd John Archibald Scott MA was vicar in 1910 when the Towngate estate paid £3 10s. yearly to the vicar for sermons and £3 15s. for repairs to the church.

Threlkeld railway station, photographed by Preston Whiteley from a Keswick-bound train approaching the platform on 27 July 1963. The line from Keswick to Penrith was to remain open until March 1972.

Threlkeld main street, c. 1918, by Alfred Pettitt. The Horse and Farrier Inn is on the left, with Mrs Jane Allinson as the licensee, and the Salutation Inn is in the background, with Mrs Sarah Hindmoor as the licensee.

'Lord Paramount' was the champion Herdwick ram for 1882 and is here seen with his owner, Robert Walker Hawell of Lonscale. Joseph Hawell wrote a classic description of the Herdwick in 1888 and among their many awards Edward Hawell won with his Herdwicks at the Royal Show at Carlisle in 1880 (see page 125).

Blease Road, Threlkeld, with more sheep and a man leaning against the wall of Sycamore House is another photograph in Pettitt's series. In 1920 James Whiteley of Vale View was the schoolmaster of the school just out of sight up the road and was also Overseer of the Poor, Clerk to the Parish Council and Secretary of the Public Rooms.

Troutbeck Moor with Blencathra in the background in the 1930s shows sheep and lambs where they dare not go today as the modern A66 has destroyed the wild beauty, replacing the rural scenes with ugly danger. This moor has a number of Roman forts, and Souther Fell in the middle distance is reputed to be haunted by an army of ghostly horsemen.

Penruddock station, with signal box, semaphore signal and the goods siding, on Preston Whiteley's journey on 27 July 1963. Again the view is from the train. Penruddock station was to last another nine years, until March 1972 when the last section of the 'C, K & P' from Keswick to Penrith was closed.

The Troutbeck Hotel at Troutbeck railway station in the 1930s, pictured by Reeds of Penrith. G.C. Sherwood advertised 'fully licensed, luncheons, teas and board residence. Petrol supplied'.

Troutbeck, c. 1900, by Brittain and Wright of Stockton-on-Tees. The road bridge over the railway and the Troutbeck Hotel are on the left, with the railway station on the right. W.G. Woolton was station master with Richard Hebson as signal man, and Mrs Elizabeth Miller was licensee at the hotel.

'The new speaker as master of the Blencathra Hunt' is the title of this photograph of James William Lowther PC, GCB, JP, LL.M (Cantab), Speaker of the House of Commons from 1905 to 1927 and MP for Penrith for thirty-eight years. As the Speaker, he is reported to have remarked to an MP that he was infallible, 'like the Pope'. He was created Lord Ullswater on his retirement in 1927 and died in 1949, aged ninety-four. He was cousin to Hugh Lowther, the 'Yellow Earl' (the last Lord Lonsdale to live in Lowther Castle). (See page 140.)

Laburnam Cottage and tea garden at Dockray on the Glen in the 1920s. 'Staying here for two days—it just reminds us of Riley's story "The Garden of Delight". We are lounging in deck chairs listening to the beck which runs by the garden,' wrote Muriel to Kathy on 11 June 1929.

The Royal Hotel, Dockray in the 1930s, when Jardine Quinney offered 'Board, Residence, Luncheons, Cumberland teas, coffee and snacks.' The petrol pump requested 'Please sound horn.'

Gowbarrow Park, Ullswater was acquired by the National Trust and officially opened in August 1908 by the master of the Blencathra pack, Speaker of the House of Commons and MP for Penrith, James William Lowther (see page 138). The assembled crowd looking elsewhere, the Union Jack over the tent and the abandoned camera and bandstand indicate the 'action' was not where the photographer was. The Speaker is reported to have spent the parliamentary recess at Hutton John, driving himself there from London and taking eighteen hours to cover 310 miles.

Viewing the beauty of Gowbarrow Park by carriage on the Pooley Bridge to Patterdale road, c. 1910. There is nothing today to say that the ancient county of Cumberland came down to Ullswater near here and that everything as far as the Eamont on the north side was in Cumberland. The thousand or so acres of parkland was owned by Henry Charles Howard Esq. DL, of Greystoke Castle, before the National Trust acquired it.

The adjoining Glencoyne Park, photographed by Lowe of Patterdale, was also in Cumberland—all the background was in Westmorland. Glencoyne, divided by the boundary of Westmorland and Cumberland, was another of Henry Howard's manors. (For more of the turn of the century magic of the Ullswater area see The Westmorland Lakes and The Eden Valley, Westmorland in this same series.

Matterdale church interior, by Lowe of Patterdale. The church dates from 1573 and was rebuilt in 1686. The Revd Henry Eldred Wood BA was vicar here in 1906, serving a population of 269 souls. This is one of the last places in Cumberland where 'bidding and laiting' was carried out on the death of a parishioner. Every house was visited to request attendance at the funeral.

The Old Coach Road to St John's in the Vale ran over Matterdale Common from Dockray. Here the postman is at St John's in the Vale, with stooks of corn in the field nearby, photographed by Pettitts about 1905. Letters for St John's were via Keswick. The post box at the vicarage was cleared at 11 a.m. on weekdays only.

St John's in the Vale is an ancient chapelry. The church was rebuilt in 1846 and altered in 1894. It is believed that there was a thirteenth-century hospital of St John which gave the valley its name. At the turn of the century the Revd Charles Dowding was the vicar and Miss Sarah Todhunter was the schoolmistress at the school next door 'attended by about thirty children'.

Fisher Place is shown as Thirlmere by R.M. Gibson of Gateshead on Tyne in this view from the turn of the century, when Mrs Grace Wilkinson offered apartments. Nearby at Dalehead was the post and money order office and savings bank run by George William Walton, farmer and postmaster, with Mrs Elizabeth Walton offering apartments.

The King's Head Inn at Thirlspot had long been a stopping place for passing coaches. It was occupied by James Easton, who had followed the late nineteenth-century Gaskarth family, when Stengal & Co. of London took this picture around 1902. The post box (cleared 3.45 p.m. daily except Sunday) and the coach ladder can be seen on the right.

The King's Head was, strangely, photographed for Pearson's Gossipy Guide with workmen doing alterations and re-roughcasting, around 1905. They called it the Thirlspot Inn and said, 'It is another old fashioned mountain hostelry, the replacement of which by a new fangled Hotel would be a matter for endless regret.' What would they think of the en-suite facilities today in what was the barn?

The Thirlmere Dam was a matter of some wonder after its erection in the 1890s. Leathes Water was sold by the Leathes family of Dalehead Hall to Manchester Corporation for this dam to be erected, raising the water level by twenty feet. Photograph by Blum & Degan in around 1905.

Coaches on the new road, which was said to be 'unnecessarily broad and substantial, and had been banked and blasted as though it was a railway'. The George Hotel coach from Penrith is followed by a Rigg's charabanc travelling towards Wythburn from Thirlspot, photographed by Pettitt in around 1910.

Motor coaches in the 1920s. Two charabancs from Lancashire are seen in the Hause Point cutting on the 'scenic route' on the west side of the reservoir where the new road was blasted through and railed off in true municipal fashion. A viewing point to see the Straining Well (see page 150) on the opposite shore was also provided. The Cecil Motors Guy charabanc TC 3718 is followed by a Model T Ford TB 6294. Reservoirs and motor vehicles—the modern age had arrived.

Two views of the bridges across Thirlmere before the work of the Manchester Corporation engineers ruined the area for ever. Brackmere, Lays Water, Leathes Water and Thirlmere were all names given to the lake in the valley. 'The shape of the lake is very curious', says a guide, 'being contracted almost opposite Dalehead Hall to the width of a river by the delta of a beck from Fisher Gill, and the strait thus formed is picturesquely spanned by a little wooden footbridge.' It has all gone today.

The 'Rock of Names' was much spoiled by the water engineers because when they tried to move it above the new water level it came to pieces. The pieces were reconstructed as a cairn by the new road 'in a direct line with its original position' on the old road. There has been a recent attempt to move the shattered pieces to the safety of the Wordsworth Museum but planners ruled they should remain at their present site. Many wonder why, as modern traffic and forestry wreck any romance at the water engineers' site.

William Baldry of Grasmere taught Alfred Pettitt all about photography in the 1850s. After Pettitt had left Grasmere for Keswick, Baldry also became the official photographer of the Manchester Corporation Water undertaking at Thirlmere. Miners working on the pipeline tunnel in the early 1890s pose for him.

Gough's Monument on Helvellyn—another of Canon Rawnsley's schemes—pictured by Lowe of Patterdale a decade or so earlier. The story of the unfortunate Quaker from Kendal who died there in 1805 and whose body was guarded by his dog until it was discovered three months later was made famous by both William Wordsworth and Sir Walter Scott. Locals wondered how the dog had survived.

Striding Edge
Helvellyn

Mayson

Striding Edge on Helvellyn by Henry Mayson points the way into Westmorland above
Patterdale. The Manchester Water Committee looked at Ullswater before they decided on
Thirlmere, but came back much later to extract water. Lord Birkett of Ulverston had a fell
named after him for preventing water extraction from Ullswater, but it was all in vain as water
was later taken after all, proving that municipal persistence pays.

The Thirlmere smash of 2 June 1908, when Burrell fairground steam engine 2979 pulling a series of showman's vans ran into the lake when the bank allegedly subsided. Driver Francis Wood and steersman Thomas Hector Allen were killed. Damages and costs were awarded against Manchester Corporation. The engine was only three months old and the road was about ten years old. 'In this photograph the engine is under the water under the van,' is written on the back of the postcard. Chaplows of Heslington took two weeks to recover it.

'The commencement of the aqueduct is marked by a castellated straining house on the right of the road which would have been built with infinitely better taste had it been less pretentious,' says Pearson's Guide. Here the workmen in the early 1890s stand proudly in front of their almost complete 'Castle'. Manchester Corporation Waterworks Department were very proud of their hydraulic wonder. It was here that a sworn opponent to the scheme, Canon Rawnsley, started the opening ceremony with a prayer, and the Bishop of Carlisle, another fierce opponent of the Corporation, ended the proceeding with a Benediction.

Wythburn church, c. 1910, by Pettitts, with the Rigg's coach to Keswick. The church was made famous by many poets, such as Gray and Coleridge. Wordsworth called it a 'modest house of prayer'. Was it this fame, or the Nags Head Inn opposite, that was the attraction on the coach trips?

The interior of Wythburn church, c. 1905, by Pettitts. The Revd Winfried Des Voeux Hill BA was vicar throughout the transformation of much of the parish into a reservoir. When his days were over in the 1920s the church was joined to that in St John's in the Vale.

Coaches at Wythburn on a busy day outside the Nags Head Inn. Note the coach ladder against the wall. At the turn of the century Edward Easton was the victualler and farmer. There was another inn called the Cherry Tree where the sheep gathering and merry nights were held but, along with 'Birkett's picturesque little post office', it was an early casualty when Manchester Corporation destroyed Wythburn 'city' and the surrounding habitations.

Quyfold, Wythburn, c. 1905. Quyfold was the home of Richard Cole and his family. In the last decade of the nineteenth century the Coles were at Hollin Brow.

The tollbar and vicarage on the roadside at Wythburn, with the church and the Nags Head in the far distance, in the mid-nineteenth century. The vicarage was built in 1862, before anyone realized that the community had less than sixty years to live.

The Nags Head, the church and the school but no sign of the lake water in this turn of the century view by Alfred Pettitt. Miss Mary Frost was the schoolmistress and the Revd W. Des Voeux Hill was the vicar. The community they served was doomed.

The encroaching lake, c. 1900, again by Pettitt. Times were changing. William Benton, the Waterworks Inspector, lived at Helvellyn House, Chris Boustead, the Road Foreman, at Low Close and Joseph Sandham, the straining well engineer, at the Cherry Tree.

The waters move ever closer in this G.P. Abraham photograph. The buildings of this village were being removed, and in the end only the church would remain. Canon Rawnsley penned yet another verse for the opening ceremony of the Waterworks scheme starting, 'Our generation pass, our names decay'.

Rigg's coaches on the Windermere to Keswick 'stage' route lasted until 1920 when they were replaced by motor coaches of the Lake District Road Traffic Company. Wythburn village as a community would not last that long. This Pettitt view from the turn of the century shows high season for all concerned as the loaded coach awaits the coachman.

Thirlmere in the late nineteenth century with the old road used by Wordsworth and his friends. Twenty feet of water now cover the fields and road. Manchester Corporation is no more and the North West Water Authority who took over have also passed away as politicians toy with society's infrastructure. What future effect on this valley's delicate balance, already much upset by the social requirement of providing water, will the desire for profit have?

Two views from surrounding fell tops show the encroaching water and the last vestiges of Wythburn. The lower picture shows the full extent of the flood in the late 1920s. The old road goes straight into the lake, while the new one skirts the new water level. Early twentieth-century Mancunians justified their work by saying they had improved the valley and went on to 'improve' the Haweswater area by adding 100 feet of water to the natural level of that lake in the 1930s. There they also demolished the ancient church.

This forlorn view by Matthews of Bradford shows the Nags Head Inn, then run by the Bainbridge family, and the water at the reservoir level. It was a gloomy end to a once thriving community. The 'Poets, Artists, Bishops and Sentimentalists' of the Thirlmere Defence Association had lost their fight.

Rigg's coaches on the summit of Dunmail Raise by Pettitts, and 'Motoring in Lakeland on top of Dunmail Raise' by Abrahams bring this book nearly to a close. The coaching days were almost over by the first decades of the twentieth century. Abraham's view of the motoring age is actually a hoax, with a completely reworked background to enhance the picture's impact.

626. MOTORING IN LAKELAND.
TOP OF DUNMAIL RAISE.
(ABRAHAM'S SERIES)

Open-top touring motor charabancs on top of Dunmail Raise. The Cumberland and Westmorland boundary at the summit was a very ancient boundary which the 1974 change to Cumbria took off the map. It was probably also the Strathclyde and Scotland boundary in the centuries before the Normans. The area of Westmorland on the other side of the pass can be found in The Westmorland Lakes volume in this series.

'A Lakeland Shepherd' by Maysons. This early twentieth-century scene from the hills around Keswick is from another age. Politicians and qualified experts in water, forestry and transport engineering have arrogantly contrived to ruin the ancient integrity of Central Lakeland in just over one hundred years. They thought their reasons were good and always, even now, know best.

Acknowledgements

The production of this book would not have been possible without the assistance in various ways of the following: Mrs Jean Marsh; Victoria Slowe, who encouraged me in the start of the series of books; Christine Strickland of the Kendal Library Local Studies collection, who helped with pictures and her vast knowledge of Lakeland material; George Dawson of Kendal for use of the N. Carradice collection; Mr Neil Honeyman of Barrow in Furness; Preston Whiteley of Kendal; John and Gill Bower of Ambleside; and finally those people of the Keswick area into whose families this book intrudes, and the many others who encourage and support me in my collection of old photographic images.